Images of Modern America

THE BOSTON MARATHON

To JOHN,

ENJOY!

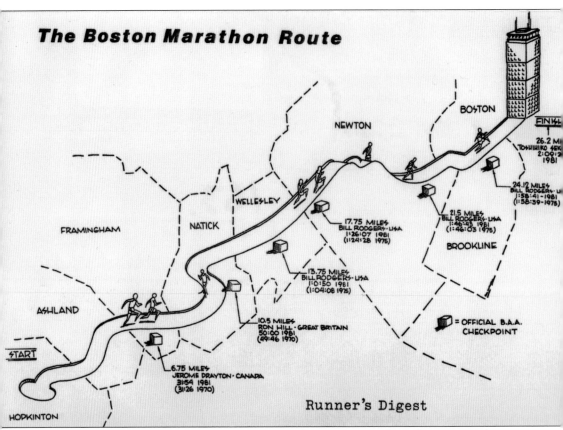

The Boston Marathon Route

BOSTON

NEWTON

FINISH
↑
26.2 Mi
TOSHIHIKO SEK
2:09:2
1981

24.12 MILES
BILL RODGERS· U
1:58:41·1981
(1:58:39·1975)

WELLESLEY

21.5 MILES
BILL RODGERS·USA
1:46:45 1981
(1:46:03 1975)

FRAMINGHAM

NATICK

17.75 MILES
BILL RODGERS·USA
1:26:07 1981
(1:24:28 1975)

BROOKLINE

13.75 MILES
BILL RODGERS·USA
1:01:50 1981
(1:04:08 1975)

ASHLAND

10.5 MILES
RON HILL·GREAT BRITAIN
50:00 1981
(49:46 1970)

= OFFICIAL B.A.A.
CHECKPOINT

START

6.75 MILES
JEROME DRAYTON·CANADA
31:54 1981
(31:26 1970)

Runner's Digest

HOPKINTON

This map from Toni Reavis's *Runner's Digest* radio program used in advertising and promotion shows a 1982 version of the course. The distance was 24.5 miles from 1897 to 1923, an incorrectly measured 26 miles and 209 yards from 1924 to 1926, a corrected 26.2 miles from 1927 to 1950, an unnoticed road-repair-shortened 26 miles and 1,232 yards from 1951 to 1956, and a correct 26.2 miles since 1957. (Toni Reavis.)

FRONT COVER: In the shadow of the Gothic Revival bell tower of Boston's Old South Church in Copley Square, runners approach the finish line on Boylston Street, near the Boston Public Library. This has been the finish since the 1986 race. (Photo by Paul Clerici.)

UPPER BACK COVER: Pictured is the start of the race in Hopkinton, with the Korean Presbyterian Church in Greater Boston in the background. (HCAM photo by Michelle Murdock.)

LOWER BACK COVER (from left to right): The *Young at Heart* statue of two-time winner (1935 and 1945) and two-time US Olympian (1936 and 1948) Johnny "The Elder" Kelley is located along the course in Newton at 19.1 miles. (Photo by Paul Clerici.) Gold-dipped olive branch wreaths, handmade in Greece, are presented to the winners. (Photo by Paul Clerici.) This colorful namesake photo op is at the Boston Marathon Expo. (Photo by Paul Clerici.)

Images of Modern America

THE BOSTON MARATHON

PAUL C. CLERICI
FOREWORD BY BILL RODGERS,
FOUR-TIME BOSTON MARATHON WINNER

ARCADIA
PUBLISHING

Published by Arcadia Publishing
Charleston, South Carolina

Printed in the United States of America

Library of Congress Control Number: 2019948662

For all general information, please contact Arcadia Publishing:
Telephone 843-853-2070
Fax 843-853-0044
E-mail sales@arcadiapublishing.com
For customer service and orders:
Toll-Free 1-888-313-2665

Visit us on the Internet at www.arcadiapublishing.com

I dedicate this book to my late parents,
Frank Clerici Sr. and Carol Hunt-Clerici; my late brother,
David Clerici; and my brother, Frank Clerici Jr.

CONTENTS

FOREWORD

The Boston Marathon became my favorite race after I moved to Boston from my hometown of Hartford, Connecticut, in 1970–1971. Though my Wesleyan University track teammate, Amby Burfoot, won Boston in 1968, the Marathon was not on national television, and I had little understanding of the event or its impact on the city of Boston. I knew Amby was training to win Boston—as I trained with him for two years at Wesleyan—yet he never really talked about his win, nor did I see his winner's medal. Amby was focused on Boston at least in part because the last American to win was his Mystic, Connecticut, high school cross-country coach, John J. Kelley, in 1957. I knew of the Olympic Marathon, as I had seen it on television in 1964 when Abebe Bikila won his second gold medal at the Tokyo Games. I was a high school junior then and couldn't even fathom ever running that far! At Wesleyan with Amby and another teammate, Jeff Galloway, who went on to become an Olympic marathoner in 1972, I began to get a feel for distance running from them.

In Boston, I had an apartment less than a mile from the finish line. Although I had quit running after graduating from Wesleyan and had become a smoker, I was still interested in track. So when Patriots' Day rolled around (a holiday unknown to me growing up in Connecticut!), my roommate and former Newington High School teammate and good friend, Jason Kehoe, and I went to see the "big race." I was astounded not only by the huge crowds surrounding the finish-line area, but also by seeing people leaning out of windows of the buildings. I could hear the roar of the crowd and the bellowing voice of the announcer at the finish line as two runners turned onto Boylston Street, running neck and neck to the finish line after the 26-mile dual. It would take me another year before I finally quit smoking and started running again. I joined the Boston YMCA and set my sights on running Boston.

I love the history of the Boston Marathon, particularly the stories of pioneers like "Bricklayer" Bill Kennedy, who won in 1917; seven-time champion Clarence DeMar; and ironman Johnny A. Kelley. Other history-making New Englanders later would include Roberta "Bobbi" Gibb, the first woman to ever run and win the Marathon, and Joan Benoit Samuelson, who went on to win the first women's Olympic Marathon gold medal in 1984. So many great New England runners, such as Patti Dillon, Bob Hall (the Marathon's first wheelchair racer and champion), Bob Hodge, Randy Thomas, Lynn Jennings, Alberto Salazar, and so on, have laced up and run Boston with outstanding performances.

I not only think of the Boston Marathon as a sporting and cultural treasure, but on par with the Indy 500, Kentucky Derby, the Masters, and the US Open. And of all these American sporting events, the Boston Marathon is by far the most international. There are really only two sports that can claim such worldwide participation and audience, and they are running and soccer.

Winning Boston truly changed my life forever! But the money was not there in the early days; it did not come until 1986, when John Hancock became the Marathon's major sponsor and supported the athletes by recognizing their excellence. Today's professional runners are more fairly compensated with prize money and appearance fees. That was not the case when I was running and winning my early marathons. However, the prize money in professional running still pales in comparison to other domestic sports. Fiscally speaking, the true beauty and high-level intensity of international competition is still not honored and respected as it should be.

In 1980, at the age of 32, I won the first-place laurel wreath and "gold" medal at Boston. The women's "winner" was Rosie Ruiz. When I spoke with her after the race, I instantly knew she had cheated. She did come close to relinquishing the gold medal, but a lone supporter of hers spoke with her and got her crying and sobbing. Soon, the media moved in, and the story of the 1980 Boston Marathon became twisted and turned to focus on this woman, who most undoubtedly had some serious mental and emotional issues. Credit should go to then–Boston Marathon race director Will Cloney for his earnest investigation and discovery of the true women's winner—Canada's Jacqueline Gareau. And to ensure that the story of Rosie's fake win didn't totally eclipse the real story of who the 1980 men's and women's champions were, he invited Jackie and myself to a ceremony to finally place the laurel wreath and gold medal with whom they rightfully belonged.

Since my first time running Boston, I've met so many people from all over the country and world that I consider good friends for life. Every distance runner aspires to run Boston—it's considered the "granddaddy" of all marathons. It was always a great honor for me to run, win, and represent my country at Boston. The level of energy and excitement at Boston is unmatched! Once you run it or watch it, you're a fan for life!

Bill Rodgers
Four-time Boston Marathon winner
Coauthor of *Marathon Man*

Acknowledgments

Running a marathon is often a solitary exercise among many. For a sport where you alone propel yourself 26 miles and 385 yards, it nevertheless still requires assistance and support along the way from many people—family, friends, and spectators. I would like to thank all those who graciously contributed photographs, provided insight, and offered never-ending support.

I would like to thank the following organizations and people: Caroline Anderson; the Association of Road Racing Statisticians (ARRS); Ashland Sporting Association (especially Steve Flynn and Steve Greenberg); Boston Athletic Association (BAA) (especially Jack Fleming, Tom Grilk, Dave McGillivray, Guy Morse III, and Gloria Ratti); Bandon Athletic Club, County Cork, Ireland (especially Billy Good); Stacia Bannerman; Bill Rodgers Running Center (especially Bill Rodgers and Charlie Rodgers); *Boston Herald*; Boston Police Department; Boston Public Library and the Digital Commonwealth (especially Bob Cullum, Leslie Jones, Danielle Pucci, and Monica Shin); Boston Red Sox (especially Matthew Thomas); Bill Boyle; Ambrose "Amby" Burfoot; City of Boston (especially Marta Crilly); Frank Clerici Jr.; Dana-Farber Marathon Challenge (DFMC) (especially Justin Knight and Jan Ross); Tom Derderian; Damian Drella; Jennifer Edwards; Fayfoto; Roberta "Bobbi" Gibb; Lee Glandorf; Hopkinton Community Access and Media (HCAM) (especially Michelle Murdock and Mike Torosian); Beverly Jaeger-Helton; Jindřich Janíček; Jeff Johnson; Kaji Aso Studio; Leo Kulinski Jr.; Barbara Lee; photograph consultant Christine Lee; Stephanie Lee; Jim Mahoney; Marco Manna; *Marathon & Beyond* (especially Rich Benyo and Jan Colarusso Seeley); Scott Mason; Roseann Sdoia Materia; Jonathan S. McElvery; McManus photorun.net; National Aeronautics and Space Administration (NASA); *New England Runner* (especially Bob Fitzgerald and Michelle LeBrun); ontarioplaques.com (especially Alan Brown); Katie Parry; Toni Reavis; Denise Robson; Jim Roy; runningpast.com (especially Andy Yelenak); Victah Sailer; Mary Kate Shea; Kathrine Switzer; Team Hoyt (especially Kathy Boyer and Dick & Rick Hoyt); Touchstone Photo; TRACS, Inc. (especially Fred Treseler III); Gigi Turgeon; 26.2 Foundation (especially Tim Kilduff); USA Track & Field (USATF); US Department of Defense (USDOD) (especially Spc. Terrence Ewings); Erin Vosgien; WBZ-TV, CBS Boston (especially Lisa Hughes); Wellesley College and the Office of Communication and Public Affairs (especially Casey Bayer and Hannah Hudson). The following publications were also helpful: *Boston Marathon: Year-by-Year Stories of the World's Premier Running Event* by Tom Derderian (Skyhorse Publishing, 2017) and *Going the Distance: Trials and Tribulations* by George C. Caner Jr. (Massachusetts Continuing Legal Education, 2001).

INTRODUCTION

The fourth marathon in the world, and second in the United States, started in Ashland, Massachusetts, by the Boston Athletic Association (BAA). Finishing in Boston as the American Marathon, Boston Athletic Association Marathon, BAA Marathon, or simply Boston Marathon, it is the oldest continually run marathon in the nation and second-oldest continually run footrace in the United States (New York's Buffalo Turkey Trot 8K started five months earlier, on Thanksgiving).

It was a child of the modern 1896 Olympic Games Marathon held April 10, where the BAA fielded one of 17 lined up in Marathon, Greece, in the second-ever marathon, the first being its qualifier. Nearly one year later—April 19, 1897—the Boston Marathon was born.

While the Boston Marathon has recorded well over a century of history, the Images of Modern America book series focuses primarily from the 1960s onward. As a result, the first six decades will certainly be represented, but the majority of this edition will be composed of the rest of the race's canon via stories, tales, and tidbits accompanying nearly 170 photographs, some never-before seen, never-before published, or extremely rare. Demarcations include the Ashland start; Hopkinton move; foreign entrants and winners; the governing body Amateur Athletic Union (AAU); inclusion of women; first wheelchair division; qualifying standards; the running boom; amateurism and professionalism; prize money; the centennial; tragedy and reclamation; and honors.

As a runner and journalist, I have been fortunate to have run Boston 23 times and covered it in the media since 1988. The combination has presented unique access and great appreciation for the race as a runner, experiencing the sights and sounds from the streets of Hopkinton to Boston, and as a journalist, writing about everything connected with its creation, building, and sustentation.

Born and raised in a Boston suburb, my interest in running and the Boston Marathon grew during the 1970s running boom. Local four-time winner Bill Rodgers was the face of the race; he won his first Boston in 1975 and his fourth and final in 1980. During those six years, the Boston leaderboard saw outstanding Americans, including Gayle Barron, Joan Benoit, Garry Bjorklund, Benji Durden, Tom Fleming, Vin Fleming, Jack Fultz, Ellison Goodall, Michiko "Miki" Gorman, Bob Hall, Bob Hodge, Don Kardong, Patti Lyons, Dick Mahoney, Kim Merritt, Kathrine Switzer, Ron Tabb, Randy Thomas, Jeff Wells, and of course, legendary two-time winner Johnny "The Elder" Kelley.

Local rooting interest came naturally with so many American greats living and training in the Boston area. The Greater Boston Track Club (GBTC), especially, which began in 1973 at Boston College, produced more Boston Marathon champions and top-10 finishers than any other club, and at times, country. GBTC stalwarts included the likes of Vin Fleming, Fultz, Hall, Hodge, Mahoney, Greg Meyer, Rodgers, Alberto Salazar, and Thomas, each of whom could be seen on any given day training on the very streets of the course.

There were also many unofficial official meeting places for these, as well as visiting, legends to congregate and gather before and after training and racing. Main spots included the Bill Rodgers Running Center stores, at which some elites worked and from where they trained, and the Eliot Hotel's famous Eliot Lounge—with its mainstay barkeep Tommy Leonard and GBTC coach Bill Squires at his "Coach's Corner," a barstool office—where runners migrated for libation and celebration.

As such, the Boston Marathon year-round permeates the city. And closer to race day, communities along the course, and those near Boston, get spruced up and decorated; television, radio, and newspapers begin showcasing stories about charity runners, volunteers, and participants; elite athletes travel to Boston to train on the course and feed off the vibe of the city; and average runners descend on the roadways in preparation for Patriots' Day.

It is, both figuratively and literally, sacred ground—figuratively, as a goal for many a marathoner who rearranges their life in order to train for a Boston Qualifier or official charity, and literally, from the deaths of Tony Nota in 1984, Humphry Siesage in 1996, and Cynthia Lucero in 2002 to the ashes of 1932 winner Paul de Bruyn scattered along the course, and to the 2013 bombings that claimed first the lives of Krystle Campbell, Lu Lingzi, and Martin Richard and then Massachusetts Institute of Technology police officer Sean Collier and Boston police officer Dennis Simmonds, and injured 265.

The Boston Marathon is more than just a footrace.

One

FROM THE BEGINNING TO THE 20TH CENTURY

It was 10 years after the BAA was established on March 15, 1887, that its 24.5-mile American Marathon was first run on Patriots' Day, which commemorates the 1775 Revolutionary War battles of Concord and Lexington.

The first 27 races began in Ashland, Massachusetts, from 1897 to 1923. Sixteen years after the universal marathon distance increased to 26.2 miles for the 1908 London Olympics, the start line for the 1924 Boston Marathon was moved to the neighboring town of Hopkinton, where it has remained since, give or take a few adjustments.

For its first 69 years (1897–1965), which this chapter covers, the Boston Marathon was a men-only race in accordance to the governing-body AAU, which did not allow women to run that distance in its races. Clarence DeMar owned this race with a record seven wins between 1911 and 1930, which included a remarkable 11-year gap between his first (1911) and second (1922) victories due to heeding doctor's orders to not run partly due to health issues. Another formidable figure was Johnny "The Elder" Kelley, who won in 1935 and 1945, along with a record seven second-place finishes. Between 1928 and 1992, he started a record 61 times and finished a record 58.

Participation remained low during these early decades, with 18 entrants in 1897 and a peak of 447 in 1965, the last year before women began to run. In fact, 1906 was the first year it reached 100 starters (105), 1928 was when it first hit 200 (with 285), and 1964 when it finally surpassed 400 (with 403).

For the first 50 years, the Boston Marathon was organized by committee, with no race director until 1947. Many traditions that began during these years continued for decades, including the single start (which ended with a separate elite women-only start in 2004, then two separate waves in 2006) and noontime gun (which ended with a 10:00 a.m. start in 2007); and some still continue, including a Brown family member as an official starter of the race (which began in 1905 with George V. Brown, who held many positions at the BAA from 1899 to 1937) and an olive branch wreath awarded to the winner (1932). Debuts also included the first American winner, non-American winner, American sweep, foreign sweep, multiple winner, military relay, Heartbreak Hill named, world-best time, BAA winner, and winners from more foreign countries.

The first Boston started at 12:19 p.m. on Patriots' Day, Monday, April 19, 1897, on Pleasant Street in Ashland, as depicted in this Robert Levine mural. Unveiled on October 24, 2016, the mural is on permanent display at Marathon Park near the original starting line. (Ashland Sporting Association.)

Runners are pictured at the Ashland Half Marathon. This race, as well as others, begins at the starting line of the original Boston Marathon. For its first two years in 1897 and 1898, the Boston Marathon started on Pleasant Street in Ashland at this very site. (Ashland Sporting Association.)

With their longstanding association with the race and the BAA, a Brown family member has started Boston every year, except for one, since 1905. The following family members have been bestowed the honor of starting the race: George Brown; Walter A. Brown; George Brown Jr.; Paul Brown; Thomas Brown, shown holding starter pistol, alongside Harold Rathburn; Walter F. Brown; George Brown's great-granddaughter Christina Walton; and Thomas Brown's widow, Rosalie Baker-Brown. (*New England Runner.*)

From left to right are Clarence DeMar, also known as "Mr. DeMarathon," and Ellison "Tarzan" Brown. DeMar won the Boston Marathon seven times, which is the record in the men's open division. Brown, a Narragansett Native American, won it in 1936 and in 1939, setting a course record (CR) of 2:28:51 and making him the first American man to run a sub-2:30. (Boston Public Library, Leslie Jones Collection.)

The BAA in 1918 held a relay during the Great War. Competing in the 25-miler were 15 teams of servicemen. Camp Devens Divisional Team won. From left to right are a 1918 official's ribbon and a baton used at the centennial relay run, which was done concurrently with the 2018 Boston. (Left, Andy Yelenak, runningpast.com; right, WBZ-TV, CBS Boston.)

From 1897 to 1923, the Boston Marathon was 24.5 miles and started in Ashland. When the universal distance increased to 26.2 miles for the 1908 Olympics, the BAA in 1924 moved the start to Hopkinton. After some miscalculations (1924–1926 and 1951–1956), it moved again to its current location when the finish changed in 1986. (Photo by Jennifer Edwards.)

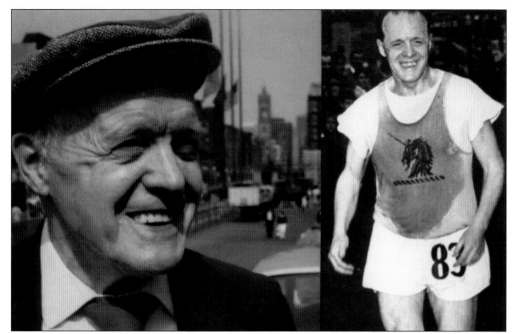

John "Jock" Semple, who first ran Boston in 1929, was a physical therapist and masseuse to professional hockey and basketball players. He also was the face of the race and fielded application requests, marshaled the runners, guarded the race's integrity, and kept the peace as he saw fit. (*New England Runner.*)

German Olympian Paul de Bruyn won in 1932 as the first non–North American. He became a US citizen, and his track club scattered his ashes along the course. Pictured in 1932 are, from left to right, de Bruyn (No. 18), William Ritola (No. 72), Hans Oldag (No. 162), and William Kyronen (No. 54). (Boston Public Library, Leslie Jones Collection.)

For the first time, in 1931, Greek-American Massachusetts state representative George Constantine Demeter linked the race to his Greek heritage. Demeter took a cue from the ancient and modern Olympic Games in Greece—whose winners received olive tree wreaths and branches—and awarded olive branch wreaths created in Greece, above, in its native green color. On a few occasions, such as during the war, the wreath had to be made locally. Most wreaths have disappeared, but four-time winner Bill Rodgers, pictured below, still has the aged crown he won in 1975, preserved in a shadow box. (Photos by Paul Clerici.)

Early fields remained low and easily manageable, as seen here around 1940. Participation first reached 100 in 1906 (105) and 200 in 1928 (285). After the lean war years, it hit 400 for the first time in 1964 (403) and 1,000 in 1968 (1,014). (Boston Public Library, Leslie Jones Collection.)

Greek Olympian Stylianos Kyriakides won in 1946 (PR 2:29:27) and used it to raise awareness and supplies for a homeland that suffered through World War II and a civil war. Pictured on the far right is Greek-American Massachusetts state representative George Constantine Demeter with the olive branch wreath. (Boston Public Library, Leslie Jones Collection.)

After 50 years of organizing the race by groups or committees, the BAA named William "Will" Cloney, pictured above with microphone at the 1994 Johnny Kelley Half Marathon in Cape Cod, Massachusetts, as the first race director in 1947. He held that position for 36 years (1947–1982), in addition to BAA president (1964–1982). Hopkinton Marathon Committee chair and 26.2 Foundation founder Tim Kilduff, pictured below, was the second race director (1983–1984). Guy Morse III was the third race director (1985–2000), and Dave McGillivray, one-time technical director, was named its fourth race director in 2001. (Photos by Paul Clerici.)

Two

WOMEN, WHEELCHAIRS, THE RUNNING BOOM, AND STAYING AMATEUR

Within this chapter's 20 years (1966–1985), several significant changes and events occurred that still resonate: women runners, Patriots' Day move, qualifying standards, wheelchair divisions, cheating, prize money, course change, international onslaught.

In 1966, Roberta "Bobbi" Gibb Bingay became the first woman to run Boston at a time when the AAU did not allow women to run that distance in its marathons. Six years later, the AAU changed its rules and the 1972 Boston Marathon saw its first official women's division. Another major change occurred for the 1970 Boston Marathon when the BAA for the first time instituted qualifying standards to reduce the number of costumed runners and those who the BAA felt were destroying the integrity of the fabled race.

In 1975, Bob Hall changed the trajectory of the Boston Marathon when he propelled himself in a wheelchair. He was promised by the BAA that if he finished under three hours he would earn an official certificate. When he finished with two minutes to spare, the push-rim wheelchair division was born.

Entrant participation began to substantially increase, which included a jump in one year from 741 in 1967 to 1,014 in 1968. And after Title IX of the Education Amendments Act of 1972 (equal federal funding for male and female sports) was passed, Frank Shorter won the 1972 Munich Olympic Marathon, Bill Rodgers won the 1975 Boston Marathon, Jim Fixx released *The Complete Book of Running* in 1977, and other related factors, the running boom contributed to a steady influx of runners nationwide, including Boston. There was also a reemergence of American champions, as 23 of the 40 combined titles were won by US runners.

The 1985 Boston Marathon also marked the end of a tumultuous era of potential financial ruin and loss of the race. In an effort to compete against other major-city marathons that offered prize money to lure elite athletes, the BAA in 1981 signed over the Boston Marathon to Marshall Medoff's International Marathons, Inc. (IMI) to solicit and attract sponsors. A subsequent three-year court case between the BAA and IMI came to an end in 1984 when the courts determined that the nonprofit BAA did not have the authority to sign over the race. As a result, the BAA retained the Boston Marathon and soon secured sponsors.

Roberta "Bobbi" Gibb Bingay, above, ran the 1966 Boston Marathon (3:21:40) as the first woman at a time when the governing-body AAU did not allow women to run that distance in its races. She also was the first female finisher in 1967 (3:27:17) and in 1968 (3:30:00). Below, at the 50th anniversary of Gibb's groundbreaking run, 2016 winner Atsede Baysa of Ethiopia, left, respected her so much that she surprised the trailblazer by presenting her with the winning trophy at the BAA Wrap-Up Media Conference, which took place the day after Baysa's 2:29:19 win. (Above, Bobbi Gibb; below, photo by Paul Clerici.)

In 1967, *Boston Traveler* photographer Harry Trask chronicled race official Jock Semple (black suit) attempting to remove Kathrine Switzer's race bib (No. 261). Semple was thwarted by Switzer's Syracuse University coach Arnie Briggs (No. 490) and her boyfriend, Tom Miller (No. 390). At the time, the AAU did not allow women to run in its marathons. (*Boston Herald.*)

From left to right are two-time winner Joan Benoit Samuelson (1979 and 1983), first official women's winner Nina Kuscsik (1972), three-time winner Sara Mae Berman (1969–1971), pioneer Kathrine Switzer, and three-time winner Bobbi Gibb (1966–1968) at a Boston Marathon centennial seminar in 1996, which was also the 30th anniversary of Gibb's first run. (Photo by Paul Clerici.)

In the final year before Patriots' Day moved to the third Monday in April, Ambrose "Amby" Burfoot won in 1968 (2:22:17) and became part of a legacy—Johnny "The Elder" Kelley befriended Johnny "The Younger" Kelley, who coached Burfoot, whose Wesleyan University roommate was Bill Rodgers. (Jeff Johnson photo courtesy Amby Burfoot.)

To reduce the number of costumed runners, unprepared athletes, and those the BAA felt destroyed the race's integrity, qualifying standards were introduced in 1970 for a certification stating, "A runner [can] . . . finish the course in less than four hours." Qualifying standards have adjusted since, but fields still include such participants. (Photos by Paul Clerici.)

Nine entrants and eight finishers were at the 1972 inaugural official women's race. This rare color photograph, taken in Hopkinton prior to the start, shows, from left to right, Nina Kuscsik, Kathrine Switzer, Elaine Pedersen, Ginny Collins, Pat Barrett, Frances Morrison (hidden), and Sara Mae Berman. Not pictured is Valerie Rogosheske. (HCAM.)

At the 40th anniversary of the 1972 Boston, when the AAU first allowed women to run in its marathons, are, from left to right, Pat Barrett (fourth), Sara Mae Berman (fifth), Kathrine Switzer (third), Valerie Rogosheske (sixth), and Nina Kuscsik (first). Not pictured are Elaine Pedersen (second), Ginny Collins (seventh), and Frances Morrison (eighth). (Photo by Paul Clerici.)

For 16 years, Dave McGillivray ran the Boston Marathon within the field of entrants. When he was hired in 1988 as the technical director, he began his streak of running the race after everyone else, usually in the late afternoon or early evening, and finishing late at night. (Dave McGillivray.)

When Bill Squires coached GBTC (1974–1984), a total of 27 runners he was coaching or had coached ran top-10 finishes, including seven wins and eight finishers as the first American at Boston. From left to right are Greg Meyer, Bob Hodge, Dick Mahoney, Squires, Alberto Salazar, Brad Hurst, and Vin Fleming. (Photo by Paul Clerici.)

Bob Hall became the first official wheelchair finisher in 1975, and later, he became the race's wheelchair athlete liaison. Champions are, from left to right, Jack Fultz, Joan Benoit Samuelson, Hall, Bobbi Gibb, Amby Burfoot, Johnny "The Elder" Kelley, Johnny "The Younger" Kelley, wheelchair athlete Jean Driscoll, Keizo Yamada, Bill Rodgers, and Greg Meyer. (Photo by Paul Clerici.)

In a new pair of running shoes mailed to him 12 days earlier by US Olympian and Nike representative Steve Prefontaine, Bill Rodgers won in 1975, setting not only a CR but also an American record (AR) of 2:09:55, pictured. "Boston Billy," who had joined the GBTC, also won in 1978, 1979, and 1980. (Bill Rodgers Running Center.)

Shown above in 2000, West Germany's Liane Winter, left, was the first foreign champion when she set the first women's division world record (WR) at 2:42:24 in 1975. Portugal's Rosa Mota, right, in the official era became the first woman to defend her title (1987 and 1988) and the first woman to win three (1990). (Photo by Paul Clerici.)

In the 1976 "Run for the Hoses," a moniker stemming from the makeshift cardboard sign affixed to the front of a lead bus that directed spectators to "hose the runners" because the temperature ranged from 90 to 100, Jack Fultz won in 2:20:19. (Photo by Scott Mason.)

As the top two Americans in 1975, winner Bill Rodgers and third-place finisher Tom Fleming were invited to run the 1976 Ohme-Hochi 30K in Japan. It was the first year Boston and Ohme participated in an annual exchange of athletes and cultures. Quinquennially since then, BAA and Ohme Athletic Association officials sign the Boston Marathon/Ohme-Hochi 30K Athlete Exchange Program extension agreement. Pictured above, from left to right, Ohme mayor Toshio Takeuchi and Joann Flaminio, the first female president of the BAA, sign the Letter of Consent of Affiliation. Additionally, cultural gifts are also presented, including handcrafted ceramics, shown below. (Photos by Paul Clerici.)

Jerome Drayton (No. 5), shown with Ron Hill (No. 1), Tom Fleming (No. 2), and Bill Rodgers (No. 14), did not finish the race in 1975. But when he won in 1977, his observations about the BAA's lack of organization and water stations, services to which he was accustomed at other races, were inevitably addressed. (Jeff Johnson photo courtesy *New England Runner.*)

Whether on the sidewalks, rooftops, front yards, beach chairs, block parties, barbecues, or between buildings, public officials estimate 500,000 spectators flood the streets of Hopkinton (pictured), Ashland, Framingham, Natick, Wellesley, Newton, Brighton, Brookline, and Boston to make the race the most "widely viewed" sporting event in New England. (Photo by Paul Clerici.)

The Red Sox have played on Patriots' Days since 1903, but the Fenway Park–Patriots' Day–Boston Marathon connection dates to 1913. The Sox began to annually play Patriots' Day home games in 1959, and morning starts commenced in 1968 so games could end in time for fans to watch the race in nearby Kenmore Square, shown below on race day. There have also been Boston Marathon–related ceremonial first pitches by, among others, Bennett Beach, who has run each year since 1968; BAA chief operating officer Jack Fleming; and AR-holder Ryan Hall with Canadian masters champion Denise Robson, pictured above in 2009. (Above, Boston Red Sox; below, photo by Damian Drella.)

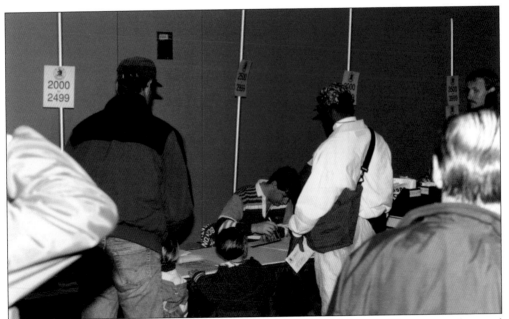

Participation remained in the dozens, hundreds, and under 1,000 for over 70 years—and around 9,000 only four years in the 1990s—so the distribution of bib numbers was easily manageable at such locales as Hopkinton High School and Sheraton Boston Hotel, pictured above. When fields grew to thousands, additional volunteers and space were required. In those decades, runners picked up numbers, depending on availability, at the John B. Hynes Veterans Memorial Convention Center on Boylston Street, pictured below; Seaport Boston Hotel and World Trade Center on the South Boston Waterfront; and the nearby Boston Convention and Exhibition Center. (Above, photo by Carol Hunt-Clerici; below, photo by Paul Clerici.)

During the running boom, the first expo set up in earnest to satisfy the needs of the runners and the public was in 1978. There, entrants picked up bib numbers, and merchants showcased new shoes, fads, souvenir shirts, and apparel. Seminars and the chance to meet famous runners at sponsor booths also debuted. Since the marathon's 1996 centennial, with its historic field of nearly 38,000, plus family members, friends, and fans of the sport, the expo for the first time expanded to three days to accommodate the masses, which is now the norm. (Photos by Paul Clerici.)

In 1979, GBTC achieved a major milestone with four of the top-10 finishers in first-place Bill Rodgers (CR/AR 2:09:27); third-place Bob Hodge (2:12:30), shown in 1986; eighth-place Randy Thomas (2:14:12); and tenth-place Dick Mahoney (2:14:36). The one-three-eight-ten finish also earned the team title. (Photo by Scott Mason.)

In a 15-year span at Boston, Joan Benoit Samuelson of Maine, pictured being interviewed by Judi Paparelli in 1997, won the race in 1979 (CR/AR 2:35:15), was third in 1981, set a WR-win in 1983 (2:22:43), was ninth in 1989, fourth in 1991, and sixth in 1993. (Photo by Paul Clerici.)

The 1980 race was marred by cheater Rosie Ruiz, pictured above at the postrace press conference with incredulous men's winner Bill Rodgers (right) after his fourth win (2:12:11). She reportedly jumped into the race at Kenmore Square, with about a mile to go, and was the first woman to cross the finish line. Doubt surfaced immediately, and the BAA, from a multiday investigation, eventually disqualified Ruiz. On April 28, at the finish line, Canadian Jacqueline Gareau (CR 2:34:28), shown at right in 1981, was rightfully crowned. (Above, Bill Rodgers Running Center; right, photo by Leo Kulinski Jr.)

For decades, the race was a television-ratings battleground when the major stations competed for viewers. CBS-TV's Boston affiliate WBZ-TV began its coverage in 1980 and is now the only local station that provides live wire-to-wire coverage. The photograph above, taken on a makeshift scaffolding set near the finish, depicts an early on-air team comprised of, from left to right, former Boston Marathon race director Tim Kilduff, US Olympic gold-medal winner Frank Shorter, coach Fred Treseler III, and trailblazer Kathrine Switzer. The photograph below, taken on the photograph bridge overlooking the finish, shows, from left to right, WBZ-TV producer Ken Tucci and anchor-host Lisa Hughes, who currently joins Switzer and Toni Reavis. (Fred Treseler III.)

Representing five Boston titles and six Olympics are, from left to right, 1957 winner and two-time US Olympian (1956 and 1960) Johnny "The Younger" Kelley; two-time winner (1981 and 1987) and two-time Japan Olympian (1984 and 1988) Toshihiko Seko; and two-time winner (1935 and 1945) and two-time US Olympian (1936 and 1948) Johnny "The Elder" Kelley. (Photo by Paul Clerici.)

Inside the Bill Rodgers Running Center store in Boston, four-time winner Bill Rodgers (1975 and 1978–1980) is pictured with three-time runner-up Patti Dillon. As Patti Lyons, she placed second in 1979 (2:38:22) and second in 1980 (2:35:08), and as Patti Catalano, she was second in 1981 with an AR of 2:27:51. (Photo by Paul Clerici.)

The 1982 "Duel in the Sun," named for its mano-a-mano hot-weather battle between winner Alberto Salazar (CR 2:08:52), foreground, and runner-up Dick Beardsley (2:08:54) was an instant classic. They also became the first pair to run sub-2:09s in the same race. (Jindřich Janíček illustration from *Fahrenheit 75*.)

Prior to organized crowd control, spectators jammed the Boston Marathon course. Charlotte Teske of West Germany, shown running between the media truck and a police motorcycle in 1982, is nearly engulfed by the crowd as she prepares to turn right onto Hereford Street to her victorious 2:29:33. (Andy Yelenak photo courtesy runningpast.com.)

Joan Benoit Samuelson, Rosa Mota, Gelindo Bordin, and Fatuma Roba have won gold medals in the Olympic Marathon and titles in the Boston Marathon. Olympic greats and champions unable to win the elusive combo include the likes of Abebe Bikila, Jim Peters, Frank Shorter, Grete Waitz (pictured), and Degage "Mamo" Wolde. (Photo by Leo Kulinski Jr.)

Greg Meyer came in 11th in 1981 (2:13:07). He then moved to Boston, worked in the Bill Rodgers Running Center, and trained with GBTC, where Bill Squires coached six of the eight winners since 1975. Pictured in 1983, Meyer won in 2:09:00. (Jeff Johnson photo courtesy *New England Runner.*)

Either at the Consulate General of Greece in Boston or the Great Hall in the Massachusetts State House, pictured above, the Consulate General of Greece in Boston has presented the made-in-Greece olive branch wreaths to the BAA since 1984. Originally in its natural green color, gold-dipped wreaths first appeared in 2006 (for *The Spirit of the Marathon* statue unveiling) and then in 2010 (for the Battle of Marathon's 2,500th anniversary). Pictured below in 2019 are, from left to right, Greek consul general Stratos Efthymiou, BAA Board of Governors president Michael O'Leary, Boston mayor Marty Walsh, Alpha Omega Council event chairman John Kopellas, and former Massachusetts governor Michael Dukakis. (Photos by Paul Clerici.)

Many notables have run, including, above, clockwise from top left, NASCAR driver Jimmie Johnson, author Jim Fixx (*The Complete Book of Running*), actor David James Elliott (*JAG*), and American Samoa Olympian Gary Fanelli (as "Elwood Blues"). Some others are authors Tom Derderian (*Boston Marathon*), Hal Higdon (*Boston*), and Erich Segal (*Love Story*); actors Valerie Bertinelli (*One Day at a Time*) and Will Ferrell (*SNL*); singers Joey McIntyre and Danny Wood (New Kids on the Block); Massachusetts governor Michael Dukakis; Boston mayor Ray Flynn; and US congressman Joseph Kennedy III. Pictured below, spectator Santa Claus waves to runners. (Clockwise from top left, photos by Paul Clerici, Leo Kulinski Jr., Paul Clerici, Paul Clerici, and Leo Kulinski Jr.)

The 1984 Boston Marathon winners, Geoff Smith (No. 1), pictured above in 1984, and Lorraine Moller, pictured at left in 1986, were also competing to qualify for their respective Olympic teams for the 1984 Summer Olympic Games. Smith won in 1984 (2:10:34) and made his Great Britain Olympic team. He also defended his title in 1985 (2:14:05). Moller also won in 1984 (2:29:28) and made her New Zealand Olympic team. She came in fifth in the inaugural 1984 Olympic Women's Marathon (2:28:54) and would later win marathon bronze at the 1992 Summer Olympic Games (2:33:59). (Above, Jim Mahoney photo courtesy *New England Runner*; left, photo by Scott Mason.)

Atop the R.H. Long Cadillac car dealership building in Framingham, located just before the 10-kilometer mark, for decades the Melchiorri's Dixieland Hobos of Natick would continually play music during the Marathon to inspire runners, and the set list would include the fan-favorite "When the Runners Come Running In," à la "When the Saints Go Marching In." (Photo by Paul Clerici.)

An unofficial sign of spring occurs in mid-March, a month before the race, on Banner Day. Four-time winner Bill Rodgers helps ceremoniously hang the first of 500 Boston Marathon street banners on city utility poles. Hopkinton also has a similar tradition where banners are hung throughout the town. (Photo by Paul Clerici.)

At a Boston Marathon press conference, from left to right are German Olympian Uta Pippig, US Olympic medalist Shalane Flanagan, US Olympian Ryan Hall, two-time World Marathon Challenge winner Rebecca "Becca" Pizzi, US Olympic medalist Joan Benoit Samuelson, US Olympian Bill Rodgers, US Olympic medalist Deena Kastor, US Olympic medalist Meb Keflezighi, and US Olympic Trials marathoner Greg Meyer. (Photo by Paul Clerici.)

Starting with the centennial, there was a great influx of instructional, directional, medical, promotional, decorative, and water-station signage along the course. But prior to the 100th, signs such as all the mile and kilometer markers could fit in one car, as seen here in 1992. (Photo by Paul Clerici.)

From 1965 to 1985, the Boston Marathon finished in a smaller area in front of the Prudential Insurance Building on Ring Road, which was parallel to Boylston Street. This 1966 photograph shows how much simpler it was then with a small staging area and a single painted line with the word "finish" to denote the end of the race. A closer look of the finish area in 1981, below, shows exposed wood panels, colorful bunting, and an uncovered photograph bridge and small bleacher section with room for only a few dozen people. (Above, City of Boston; below, photo by Paul Clerici.)

Shown in 1987, in front of the Old South Church in Copley Square, is a colorful display of runners, located a few blocks from the finish. A benefit of John Hancock Mutual Life Insurance Company funding was more signage such as this. (Photo by Paul Clerici.)

Pictured is Boylston Street. At the top left-hand corner is the fire station at the Hereford Street turn, and the large rectangle-shaped cement patio on the left is the former site of the Ring Road finish from 1965 to 1985. The yellow line at the bottom right-hand corner is the finish line beginning in 1986. (Photo by Paul Clerici.)

Three

MONEY AND THE WORLD

This chapter features the expansion and growth fed by John Hancock Mutual Life Insurance Company's initial 10-year, $10 million principal sponsorship in 1986.

After 89 years as an amateur race, the Boston Marathon turned professional. The results were immediate and significant, with a steady increase of international talent (and African dominance), media attention, sponsorships, signage, fast results (sub-2:06 times and a world-best 2:03:02), world-class status, charity runners, year-round BAA races, and real-time in-race data for the massive television coverage and interest. Some of the greatest changes to the race, such as start times, separate waves and starts, on-course amenities, the finish line, and more, also occurred in these decades.

The mammoth 100th anniversary edition of the Boston Marathon was celebrated in 1996 and featured the world's largest marathon field and other centennial highlights (see Chapter 4).

The Boston Marathon also expanded its reach in several other areas. Apparel, souvenirs, films, documentaries, and books were just some of the items that helped promote and celebrate the race. Environmentally friendly vehicles, educational programs, charity runners, and youth races greatly benefited the communities. And in addition to the increase in participation, from 4,904 entrants in 1986 to an estimated field of 31,500 in 2020, the race reached far beyond the confines of the local roads with concurrent "shadow runs" overseas at military bases and even in orbit more than 200 miles above the course. It also joined with major-city marathons in London, Berlin, Chicago, New York, Tokyo, and the Olympics and International Association of Athletics Federations (IAAF) World Championships, to form the point-based World Marathon Majors series. And it hosted the US Olympic Women's Marathon Trials in 2008.

These decades also included a drug-tested title disqualification and the fatal tragedy from the explosion of two bombs during the 2013 race. For the first time in its history, the Boston Marathon, a target of homegrown terrorism, was prematurely stopped with runners still on the course. Near the Boylston Street finish, three spectators were killed and 265 others injured. As part of the subsequent manhunt, two law enforcement officers died, one suspect was killed, and one suspect was captured. The bombings resulted in a new norm of security measures at events worldwide. But Boston Strong prevailed to reclaim the race and the city.

For its 1986 race, the BAA and John Hancock Mutual Life Insurance Company agreed to a $10 million principal sponsorship deal, which ensured financial backing, prize money, and other funding for 10 years. As of the 2019 race, whose prize money totaled $871,000, nearly $21 million has been awarded since that first year. The 1986 race was won by Robert de Castella of Australia (CR 2:07:51), pictured above, who earned $60,000 for the win, CR, and bonuses; and Ingrid Kristiansen of Norway (2:24:55), pictured at left, who won $30,000 for the win. (Above, Victah Sailer/McManus photorun.net courtesy *New England Runner*; left, photo by Scott Mason.)

The Spotters Network, from the Race SpotWatch division of sports marketing and event management group TRACS, Inc., began in 1986 by Tim Kilduff and Fred Treseler III. Trained students on the course mark, record, and phone in mile splits, as demonstrated above by, from left to right, Hannah Greenberg, Isabelle Tambascio, and Grace Seta recording Kenya's Wesley Korir at a mile marker. That data is received by volunteers at the WBZ-TV, CBS Boston studio, shown below, who also track the progress of the races within the race, via monitors, and then disseminates the information to its live wire-to-wire television broadcast. (Fred Treseler III.)

For the first time in 1989, the John Hancock Elite Athletes' Village, located a few blocks from the finish, housed the world's best. A small army of volunteers coordinated everything involved with hosting national and international athletes, including course tours, massages, food (specialized to foreign diets), training, downtime, and tourism. The Boiler Room, a central command center, pictured above, is where everything flowed to monitor each athlete and requirement throughout their time before, during, and after the race. No detail went unnoticed, such as updated whiteboards of flight arrivals and departures, pictured below, for all the athletes, coaches, agents, trainers, and family members. (Photos by Paul Clerici.)

After only one charity in 1977, it was through the John Hancock Nonprofit Program (which began in 1986), BAA Charity Program (1989), and others, that an all-time fundraising record of $38.7 million from 2,500 participants for 297 charities was set in 2019. One such benefactor is the Dana-Farber Marathon Challenge, pictured above. (DFMC, Justin Knight Photography.)

In 1981, Dick Hoyt and his son Rick, born with cerebral palsy and diagnosed as a spastic quadriplegic, the founding members of Team Hoyt, participated in their first of 32 Bostons. In 1990, Pres. Ronald Reagan invited them for a visit, shown here; from left to right are brothers Russell and Rick; father, Dick; and President Reagan. (Team Hoyt.)

Boston Marathon race director Guy Morse III (left) spearheaded a deal with Adidas that put official race apparel at the expo and in stores. Also helping with the announcement are 1990 WR-setting (2:11:04) masters champion John Campbell of New Zealand (center) and US Olympian and Adidas rep Pete Squires. (Fayfoto courtesy *New England Runner*.)

Pictured in 1991, Kenya's Ibrahim Hussein (right) won Boston in 1988, 1991, and 1992. His first victory began the dominance of African winners, which includes 28 of the next 32 men's winners from either Kenya (22) or Ethiopia (6). Also shown are Ireland's Andy Ronan (left) and Mexico's Alejandro Cruz. (*New England Runner*.)

To "carbo-load" the runners, prerace pasta parties have been held at various locations, including the World Trade Center in the Seaport District and City Hall Plaza in Boston. Shown in 2004 serving the pasta are, from left to right, race director Guy Morse III and Boston mayor Tom Menino. (City of Boston.)

After years of elite athletes being forced to breathe hazardous exhaust fumes from lead vehicles, the 1991 Boston Marathon vehicles ran on natural gas for the first time—thanks to the local Boston Gas Company. Shown with the new vehicles in Copley Square is four-time winner Bill Rodgers. (*New England Runner.*)

The John Hancock Scholars & Stars Program, which began in 1993, takes place at the Elmwood Elementary School in Hopkinton. Throughout the school year, students learn about the culture, arts, and language of Kenya. Four days prior to the race, dignitaries, teachers, race officials, and students meet the elite Kenyan athletes who are introduced at the gym with much fanfare, dry ice, music, spotlights, and cheers, above. The gym is also decorated with Kenyan scenes and sayings created by the students, who also wear Kenya-flag T-shirts and wave the African nation's colors, below. (Michelle Murdock photos courtesy HCAM and 26.2 Foundation.)

The BAA in 1997 started the BAA Relay Challenge for middle school students to get the chance to run on Boylston Street. Part of the year-long Training Basics program includes coaching in setting goals, pacing, and teamwork. This 2005 photograph shows participants from Walpole, Massachusetts, in Copley Square. (Photo by Paul Clerici.)

Pictured at left is Ethiopia's Fatuma Roba in 1998. She won three consecutive Boston Marathons (1997–1999) and started African women's dominance, as 20 of the next 23 women's titles were won by either a Kenyan (12) or Ethiopian (8). Pictured at right is Kenya's Margaret Okayo at her 2002 win (CR 2:20:43). (Left, *New England Runner*; right, *New England Runner*, Jonathan S. McElvery.)

In 2002, the BAA and City of Boston began to jointly present the Patriots' Award to a "New England–based individual, group, or organization that is patriotic, philanthropic, and inspirational, and fosters goodwill and sportsmanship." Boston Patriot Ron Burton Sr., the 2004 recipient, at the 2002 Olympic Torch Relay. (Photo by Paul Clerici.)

Elite women enjoyed their first separate start in 2004 at 11:31 a.m. This 2012 photograph shows the top women in their barricaded walkway to the start. To their left is the Main Street Cemetery, through which the elites traversed from their prerace basement enclave inside the former First Congregational Church. (Photo by Paul Clerici.)

For victories, wheelchair athlete Ernst van Dyk, pictured with BAA Board of Governors president and chief executive officer Tom Grilk (right), leads with 10, followed by wheelchair athlete Jean Driscoll with 8; runner Clarence DeMar with 7; wheelchair athlete Candace Cable-Brookes with 6; and wheelchair athletes Jim Knaub, Tatyana McFadden, and Wakako Tsuchida with 5 apiece. (Photo by Paul Clerici.)

The first Boston Marathon "shadow run" on foreign military bases was in 2005. US Air Force major Harland Peelle, pictured, breaks the tape at Contingency Operating Base in Adder, Iraq, on April 18, 2009. (US Department of Defense, Spc. Terrence Ewings, 4th Brigade Combat Team, 1st Cavalry Division Public Affairs.)

At left, ultramarathoner Dean Karnazes (left, center) is seen running the Boston course in October 2006 for his 50 marathons in 50 states in 50 consecutive days. Earlier in the year, the point-based World Marathon Majors series started with Boston, London, Berlin, Chicago, New York, Tokyo (2012), Olympics, and IAAF World Championships. Pictured at right is the Six-Star Finisher medal for those who run all six big-city marathons. (Photos by Paul Clerici.)

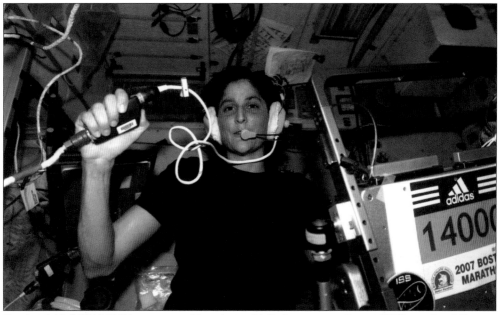

On April 16, 2007, NASA astronaut, Expedition 14 flight engineer Sunita Williams "ran" Boston tethered to a treadmill aboard the International Space Station (ISS) 210 miles above the course. In 4:23:10, she became the first to run a marathon in space. She circled Earth nearly three times as the ISS flew five miles per second. (NASA.)

The 2008 US Olympic Women's Marathon Trials was run the morning before the Boston Marathon, on Sunday, April 20, through the streets of Boston and Cambridge. It started on Boylston Street in the shadow of the John B. Hynes Veterans Memorial Convention Center (above) and concluded at the redressed finish line (below). The top three finishers, Deena Kastor, Magdalena Lewy Boulet, and Blake Russell, made the US Olympic team. The oldest entrant was 50-year-old Joan Benoit Samuelson, winner of the inaugural women's trials and marathon in 1984, and she came in 90th out of 124 finishers. (Photos by Paul Clerici.)

Between 2001 and 2011, the BAA created the BAA Half Marathon (2001), BAA Invitational Mile (2009), BAA 5K (2009), and BAA 10K (2011). The 5K, 10K, and half-marathon comprise the BAA Distance Medley race series, wherein participants compete with combined results. For the BAA Invitational Mile, the course includes a portion of the Boston Marathon's Boylston Street finish; here, above, the men turn left off Exeter Street in 2009. Shown at the start of the inaugural women's mile, below, are, from left to right, Marina Muncan, Anna Willard, Shalane Flanagan, Amy Mortimer, Carrie Tollefson, and Michelle Sikes—all world-class athletes. (Photos by Paul Clerici.)

At the first Boston Marathon in 1897, Wellesley College students cheered Harvard University runner Richard Grant, and an annual (except one year when it was held during Easter break) tradition was born. The thunderous support was nicknamed the "Scream Tunnel" because they used to line up on both sides of the runners near Cazenove Hall, as depicted here in 1983, above. Starting in 2011, students began to field requests for signs for the barricades with the help of social media. It takes weeks to create the signs, below. (Above, Wellesley College Archives, Library and Technology Services; below, Wellesley College Office for Communication & Public Affairs.)

Guy Morse III (far right) was honored in 2010 for 25 years of service in a variety of roles at the BAA. From left to right are BAA Board of Governors president and chief executive officer Tom Grilk, 1990 winner Gelindo Bordin, 1985 winner Lisa Larsen-Weidenbach, 1984–1985 winner Geoff Smith, and 1980 winner Jacqueline Gareau. (Photo by Paul Clerici.)

The 2011 race was the fastest Boston, as the top-10 men all finished under 2:09:00. From left to right, Robert Kiprono Cheruiyot was 6th (2:06:43), Robert Kipchumba was 10th (2:08:44), Ryan Hall was 4th and set an American CR (2:04:58), and Geoffrey Mutai won in a World Best/CR (2:03:02). (Photo by Scott Mason.)

On Boylston Street at the 2013 Boston Marathon, two bombs exploded that killed 3 spectators and injured 265. The area was closed as a crime scene while investigators searched for evidence, above. Services were held throughout the days and weeks that followed, including the "Healing Our City: An Interfaith Service" at the Cathedral of the Holy Cross in Boston on April 18, below. Attendees included, from left to right, Pres. Barack Obama, First Lady Michelle Obama, Massachusetts governor Deval Patrick, First Lady of Massachusetts Diane Patrick, First Lady of Boston Angela Menino, and Boston mayor Tom Menino. (Above, photo by Paul Clerici; below, City of Boston.)

On April 20, 2013, Red Sox player David Ortiz, during pregame ceremonies at the first post-bombings game at Fenway Park, made an emotional emphatic proclamation to reclaim Boston. The team has recognized those touched by the tragedy, including first responders, survivors, victims, their families, and law enforcement. Above is survivor Roseann Sdoia Materia, who lost her leg, with her firefighter husband, Mike Materia, who she met when he helped save her life. She is seen hugging Boston police commissioner William Evans. Pictured below is Meb Keflezighi after he won in 2014 (2:08:37). (Above, Boston Red Sox, Matthew Thomas; below, Tim Kilduff.)

New England weather on Patriots' Day has seen it all—snow, rain, mist, and even a solar eclipse. Pictured above in 2002, the Athletes' Village is barely visible in the heavy mist that blanketed the area. The mist forced the cancellation of the flyover and grounded helicopters for most of the day, resulting in limited television coverage to mostly street-level cameras because no choppers meant no ability to bounce back the television signal. Below, a steady cold and windswept rainstorm accompanied runners in 2018, as a strong headwind also hampered the comfort level and affected those from warmer climates. (Photos by Paul Clerici.)

Dangerous heat has greeted many Patriots' Days. Above, water stations at the Natick Fire Department were available in 2012. That year, the BAA issued the unprecedented prerace announcement that entrants could defer to 2013 if they felt uncomfortable running in 80- and 90-degree temperatures. Below, 2019 saw rain, humidity, heat, sun, and then more rain later in the race, which resulted in some runners struggling to finish, including US Marine Micah Herndon, who ran to honor Marine Matthew Ballard, journalist Rupert Hamer, and Marine Mark Juarez, who all died from an improvised explosive device on their 2010 convoy in Afghanistan that Herndon survived. (Photos by Paul Clerici.)

A subculture of unofficial "bandits," unregistered runners who ran without a number, populated the back of the pack. The Red Snakes, whose red banner is shown at the finish, waited and awarded colorful certificates. The brainchild of Kaji Aso, they were named after a symbol of inspiration. (Photo by Paul Clerici.)

Since it added the wheelchair category at the 1975 Boston Marathon, the BAA endeavors to accommodate diversity. This includes starts for men's wheelchair, women's wheelchair, noncompetitive hand cycle and duo participants, and "competitive divisions for classified ambulatory Para athletes—vision, lower limb, upper limb impairments." (Photo by Scott Mason.)

Close finishes have included zero seconds (2000 men), one second (1988 men and 2009 women), two seconds (1978, 1982, and 2019 men and 2008, 2011, and 2012 women). Pictured is the 2019 final stretch near the finish line with, from left to right, winner Lawrence Cherono of Kenya (2:07:57) and runner-up Lelisa Desisa of Ethiopia (2:07:59). (Photo by Paul Clerici.)

Pictured in 2019, Ethiopia's Worknesh Degefa (2:23:31) receives the championship trophy from BAA Board of Governors vice president, secretary, historian, and archivist Gloria Ratti, a Boston Marathon treasure. Looking on are, from left to right, BAA Board of Governors president and chief executive officer Tom Grilk, Massachusetts governor Charlie Baker, and John Hancock Financial Services assistant vice president Robert Friedman (behind Ratti). (Photo by Paul Clerici.)

Four

WATERSHED CENTENNIAL

The 100th anniversary of the Boston Marathon in 1996 was a time to look back, to celebrate, and to look ahead. The centennial of the oldest annually continually run marathon garnered worldwide attention.

All eyes from the running world were on Boston. The largest field prior to 1996 was 9,629 in 1992 and 9,416 in 1995. The BAA recognized the great interest and increased the field to 38,000 (officially 38,708 entrants), which was the largest in the world. Even a first-time non-qualifying lottery was instituted to accommodate extra runners.

The centennial was also an opportunity to recognize the many contributors, administrators, and officials who kept the race alive since 1897 and the past champions and notables who became the faces of the race over the past 10 decades (reportedly all but 9 of the surviving 59 champions took part).

As a result of the magnitude of the event, which went beyond being simply a road race, the BAA needed to create several mechanisms for better accommodating not only the 38,708 entrants, but also an estimated 1.5 million spectators, 1,500 media, and 10,000 volunteers. It was a massive multi-municipality undertaking that stretched to the maximum communities, manpower, infrastructure, media, medical, responders, administrators, and execution.

Many initiatives are still used, such as the Athletes' Village at Hopkinton High School for all the runners; an expanded expo, which grew to three days; a larger pasta party, whose venue moved to City Hall Plaza; additional press conferences and seminars, which stretch over several days; signage, stations, and barricades at the start, finish, and throughout the course; electronic chip timing by ChampionChip, which was first introduced at Boston; tamper-proof bibs that featured a hologram design; organizational backups and procedures, which have been expanded upon as needs arose; youth events that are now year-round and include educational and health benefits; and more.

The success of the centennial also revealed what limits the BAA and communities along the course could handle. The main result was field size, which slowly grew from 10,471 entrants the following year (1997) to 17,813 in 2000 and 20,223 in 2003 to 25,283 in 2008 before averaging 30,000 beginning in 2015. It also enabled the BAA to increase the entrant field to 35,671 for the post-bombing year in 2014 that also included many of the 5,633 athletes who were stranded on the course in 2013.

For the centennial race, marketing reached new heights in terms of merchandising with shirts, jackets, hats, jewelry, posters, ornaments, cereal boxes, stamps, and more. One of the most colorful and practical items was the Mylar blanket runners received, which also featured the names of all previous winners. (Photo by Paul Clerici.)

Chip-timing technology was used for the first time to record the largest marathon field in the world. ChampionChip transponders on runners' shoes recorded times when running over mat-covered antennas. At the expo, volunteers Rich Seale (left) and Paul Fucile, of South Boston's L Street Running Club, test ChampionChips. (Photo by Paul Clerici.)

To accommodate worldwide interest for the 100th, greater organized press events were orchestrated for the 1,500 media personnel from 300 outlets, second only to the NFL Super Bowl. Events already being held over the years were expanded, and there was an increase in additional press conferences, some of which are still held. The John Hancock Elite Athlete Press Conference, pictured above in 2011, begins with opening remarks with the world's best onstage. Afterward, the athletes disperse throughout the rooms to answer questions, as seen below in 1995 with Boston sportswriter Joe Concannon (center) interviewing Cosmas Ndeti. (Photos by Paul Clerici.)

The BAA Champions Breakfast started in 1996 with bib number photo ops and question-and-answer sessions with former and current champions. Pictured in 2011 from left to right are BAA Board of Governors president and chief executive officer Tom Grilk, four-time winner Catherine Ndereba, 2010 winner Robert Kiprono Cheruiyot, 2010 winner Teyba Erkesso, and interpreter Sabrina Yohannes. (Photo by Paul Clerici.)

Pictured is the BAA Boston Marathon Champions' Trophy. At left is the silver top portion presented to the winners at the finish line. For the rest of the year, the top portion of the trophy sits atop its large engraved wooden base, which is on permanent display at the BAA office in Boston when not traveling elsewhere. (Photos by Paul Clerici.)

Boston Marathon champions pictured above from left to right are (first row) Johnny Miles, Paavo Kotila, Paul de Bruyn, Kee Yong Ham, Shigeki Tanaka, Morio Shigemitsu, and Keizo Yamada; (second row) Johnny "The Elder" Kelley, Johnny "The Younger" Kelley, Alvaro Mejia, Greg Meyer, Jack Fultz, Charlotte Teske, Gelino Bordin, and Sara Mae Berman; (standing) Neil Cusack, Jacqueline Gareau, Joan Benoit Samuelson, Amby Burfoot (behind Samuelson), Ron Hill, Dave McKenzie, Robert de Castella, Geoff Smith, Lisa Larsen-Weidenbach, Liane Winter, Nina Kuscsik, and Gayle Barron. Pictured below from left to right are (first row) Kee Yong Ham, Shigeki Tanaka, Morio Shigematsu, Keizo Yamada, Hideo Hamamura, Kenji Kimihara, Yoshiaki Unetani, and Veikko Karvonen; (second row) Greg Meyer, Jack Fultz, Charlotte Teske, Gelindo Bordin, Sara Mae Berman, Olavi Suomalainen, Eino Oksanen, and Jacqueline Hansen; (standing) Robert de Castella, Geoff Smith, Lisa Larsen-Weidenbach, Liane Winter, Nina Kuscsik, Gayle Barron, Allison Roe, Ingrid Kristiansen, Miki Gorman, Jon Anderson (behind Gorman), Olga Markova, and Loraine Moller. (Photos by Paul Clerici.)

The first Athletes' Village was created in 1996 behind Hopkinton High School, shown above. According to the BAA, there were over 75,000 entry requests, 24,000 who qualified, 5,000 from the one-time open lottery, and over 800 buses to transport participants. The dogged New England winter continued into April with 15 inches of new-fallen snow in Hopkinton five days prior to the start and heavy rain two days before, leaving a natural mess on the field. However, breakneck snow removal, impromptu drainage, and helicopters hovering above the field to dry the grass all led to acceptable, albeit somewhat muddy, conditions, pictured below. (Photos by Paul Clerici.)

It took only 28 minutes, 32 seconds for the record field of 36,748 participants to cross the starting line. Released first were elite and qualified entrants corralled on Main Street from the starting line to Hayden Rowe Street, followed by the next section of qualified runners from Hayden Rowe Street, pictured above at left, with the next section of runners on Main Street waiting their turn. The final side street, Grove Street, was utilized with the lottery field. Below, runners pass by the starting line staging, which included, among others, starter US senator John Kerry, second from left. (Photos by Paul Clerici.)

African dominance continued in 1996 with, from left to right, Kenyan Joseph Kamau (twenty-ninth), Kenyan Charles Tangus (seventh), Ethiopian Abebe Mekonnen (sixth), Kenyan Cosmas Ndeti (third), Kenyan Moses Tanui (first), Kenyan Lameck Aguta (fourth). In the centennial win, Tanui beat former recent champions Ndeti, Aguta, and Mekonnen. (Bill Boyle Touchstone Photo courtesy *New England Runner.*)

After covering 25.2 miles, runners enter Kenmore Square where it is duly painted on the road that there is reassuringly only "One Mile To Go." Shown in 1996, runners eye the John Hancock Tower, which marks the finish line, as an inflatable Ronald McDonald looks down from the rooftops. (Photo by Paul Clerici.)

According to the BAA, 97.6 percent of the 36,748 starters finished (35,868). Official timing was extended to eight hours to be considered an official finisher. And the post-finish area of baggage buses, medals, changing tents, and so on stretched six-tenths of a mile to the Boston Common, located four blocks away. (Photo by Frank Clerici Sr.)

Shown as defending champions, from left to right, Germany's Uta Pippig (2:27:12) and Kenya's Moses Tanui (2:09:15) won the centennial. Pippig battled physical maladies to come from behind to win her third title. Tanui, who halted Cosmas Ndeti's attempt at win number four, bested his runner-up place from the year before. (Photo by Paul Clerici.)

The BAA Wrap-Up Media Conference is held the day after the race. At far right, holding large checks representing their 2018 winnings, are champions Desiree Linden (left) and Yuki Kawauchi; standing, directing the media, is BAA chief operating officer Jack Fleming. (Photo by Paul Clerici.)

Also of note in 1996 was the closing of the Eliot Lounge, located in the Eliot Hotel. The bar was *the* go-to place for runners. Barkeep Tommy Leonard kept tabs on athletic records (some painted on the premises), winners' national anthems, walls of running mementos, and endless stories. (Photo by Paul Clerici.)

Five

MOMUMENTS, STATUES, AND HONORS

The Boston Marathon has been honored, celebrated, and recognized in many ways. Tangible honors—monuments, statues, plaques—appear mostly in and around the course itself, but also throughout the world. Some are celebratory; some are for healing.

The most concentrated locations are in Massachusetts, near the start areas in Ashland and Hopkinton and the finish area in Boston. Ashland is where the Boston Marathon started its first 27 races (1897–1923) and is home to Marathon Park and its monuments at the site of the inaugural race. Hopkinton, where the race has started since 1924, has many statues and monuments that recognize such figures as longtime BAA official George V. Brown, the inspirational father-son Team Hoyt duo of Dick and Rick Hoyt, two-time winner Johnny "The Elder" Kelley, several Korean champions, 1946 winner Stylianos Kyriakides, and soon three-time winning pioneer Roberta "Bobbi" Gibb. Boston is home to the Boston Marathon Centennial Monument in Copley Square and two memorials on Boylston Street that honor the victims and survivors of the 2013 bombings. And along the course, there's the Johnny "The Elder" Kelley statue, Boston Strong Bridge, and Official Greeter of the Boston Marathon Tommy Leonard Bridge.

Off the course, there's the Bill Rodgers bronzed running shoes at Faneuil Hall in Boston; Clarence DeMar monument in Melrose, Massachusetts; Johnny "The Elder" Kelley statues, trails, and parks in Cape Cod, Massachusetts; Johnny "The Younger" Kelley statue in Connecticut; three-time winner Leslie "Les" Pawson plaque in Rhode Island; Joan Benoit Samuelson statues in Maine; and Rodgers and Samuelson statues in Iowa.

Internationally, Boston winners are national heroes. Canada honors two-time winner Johnny Miles with statues, festivals, and races, and 1907 winner Thomas Longboat with plaques and statues; Guatemala salutes 1952 winner Doroteo Guamuch Flores with a namesake stadium, bridge, roadway, and statue; Greece has three statues of Kyriakides; and Ireland features a monument for 1903 winner John Lordan and a statue of 1908 runner-up Johnny Hayes.

Memorials for the 2013 bombing victims include the Krystle Campbell Peace Garden in Medford, Massachusetts; the Martin Richard "No More Hurting People . . . Peace" statue at Bridgewater State University, and Martin's Park in Boston; Officer Sean Collier Memorial at MIT; and a memorial at each Boylston Street site that recognizes all five victims and 265 survivors, and three permanent painted blue lines at the start and finish.

Here is the original "It All Started Here in 1897" sign, created by Ashland Historical Society member Richard Fannon. For decades before the resurgence of Marathon Park, it was the only indicator that marked the location of the original starting line on Pleasant Street in Ashland. (Ashland Sporting Association.)

Marathon Park's first phase, dedicated June 21, 2003, included the Keepers of the Flame monument. Six years earlier, it was the idea of Ashland High School seniors Don Keilson and Michael Meade, who received support from historian David Foster. It recognizes Bob Campbell, Scottie McFetridge, Jerry Nason, Tony Nota, and Jock Semple. (Photo by Paul Clerici.)

Before the Boston Marathon moved to Hopkinton, the first 27 years (1897–1923) started in three separate locations in Ashland. The unveiling of Marathon Park at the original site (above) occurred on October 26, 2013, with, from left to right, Ashland town official Jon Fetherston, Massachusetts state senator Karen Spilka of Ashland, and BAA Board of Governor Guy Morse III presenting the Lou Mancini–created sign. A new wooden walkway and six informational plaques that display the history of the race in Ashland were also unveiled. Pictured below are, from left to right, BAA Board of Governors chief executive officer Tom Grilk and four-time winner Bill Rodgers. (Photos by Paul Clerici.)

The iconic "It All Starts Here" sign at the Hopkinton Town Common was designed and displayed by the Hopkinton Marathon Committee in 1979. Pictured in 2003, US Olympic Marathon gold-medal winner Frank Shorter is seen resting before running the marathon while wearing a microphone for local television coverage. (Photo by Paul Clerici.)

Coinciding with the centennial, Hopkinton declared April 6, 1996, which fell on the weekend before the race, as Johnny Kelley Day for the two-time US Olympic marathoner and two-time Boston champion. One of the honors for Kelley was the naming of where Hopkinton Town Common sidewalks intersect as Johnny Kelley Crossing. (Photo by Paul Clerici.)

In 2008, the Flame of the Marathon Run arrived in Hopkinton for the Boston Marathon. Originating at the Tomb of the Athenians in Marathon, Greece, it was transported to the United States by international dignitaries. The flame was presented at press conferences the weekend of the race by Marathon mayor Spiros Zagaris, pictured above holding the protective container. Also shown are running coach Bill Squires, seated; consul general of Greece in Boston Constantinos Orphanides, second from right; and 1946 Boston winner Stylianos Kyriakides's son Dimitri Kyriakides. Below, the flame is on display in Hopkinton Town Common at the 2008 Boston Marathon. (Photos by Paul Clerici.)

This photograph, taken in Hopkinton, shows the Michael Alfano–created *The Starter* statue of longtime race starter George V. Brown, Marathon Way's street sign, and the BAA office, where in the front-center window a large unicorn cutout slowly appears as the race gets closer, finally revealing itself in full on Marathon Monday. (Photo by Paul Clerici.)

At Hopkinton's Korean Presbyterian Church in Greater Boston is a monument commemorating the 100th anniversary of Korean immigration. The Douglas Duksoo Wohn–designed honor, dedicated in 2004, recognizes top-Korean runners Yun Chil Choi, Kee Yong Ham, Bong Joo Lee, Ki Yoon Song, and Yun Bok Suh. (Photo by Paul Clerici.)

Dick Hoyt and his son Rick Hoyt, who was born with cerebral palsy and diagnosed as a spastic quadriplegic, are honored with a Mike Tabor–created *Yes You Can* statue. It was dedicated in 2013 at the former Center School on Ash Street in Hopkinton, about a block from the start. (Photo by Paul Clerici.)

In 2019, three thin blue lines honoring the three bombing victims were painted along the first mile of the Boston Marathon course. Here, a Hopkinton police officer stops traffic for tourists to take photographs near the blue lines, which begin at the letter T of the starting line. (Photo by Paul Clerici.)

Greece Olympian Stylianos Kyriakides, the 1946 Boston champion, is honored with *The Spirit of the Marathon* statue at Mile 1 in Hopkinton. Above, Kyriakides, at left, is depicted running alongside the "spirit" of fellow Greek Spiridon Louis, winner of the 1896 modern Olympic Games. It was dedicated in 2006, two years after an identical statue was dedicated in Marathon, Greece. Below, a detail shows horned demigod Pan, who legend says aided the Athenians over the Persians, and Pheidippides, the legendary mythological Greek messenger runner. Kyriakides also has statues in Statos-Agios Photios, Cyprus, and Filothei, Greece. (Photos by Paul Clerici.)

Three years after the bombings, in 2016, Boston Strong, coined by Emerson College students Christopher Dobens and Nicholas Reynolds, was painted on the Bowker Overpass bridge, pictured above, along the course between Kenmore Square and Massachusetts Avenue, where hundreds of runners were stranded on that day, April 15, 2013. Shown here are race officials clearing the course on the morning of the Marathon. (Photo by Damian Drella.)

In 1982, the Massachusetts Avenue bridge was renamed Tommy Leonard Bridge in honor of the Official Greeter of the Boston Marathon and Falmouth Road Race founder. Participants now run underneath it. (Photo by Paul Clerici.)

The day before the 1993 Boston Marathon, the *Young at Heart* statue, brainchild of Dr. Wayman Spence, was dedicated in honor of two-time winner Johnny "The Elder" Kelley. Above, at the unveiling are, from left to right, four-time champion Bill Rodgers, sculptor Rich Muno, Dr. Spence, Kelley, BAA Board of Governor Guy Morse III, BAA president Thomas Whelton (blocked, behind Morse), John Hancock Mutual Life Insurance Company president William Boyan III, and three-time winner and defending champion Ibrahim Hussein. Located along the course in Newton is the original site of the statue at the northeast corner of Commonwealth Avenue and Walnut Street, pictured below. (Photos by Paul Clerici.)

After the *Young at Heart* statue was dedicated in 1993, an errant driver damaged the sculpture, which depicts Johnny "The Elder" Kelley. After repairs, the statue was reinstalled across the street at the northwest corner of Commonwealth Avenue and Walnut Street, pictured above, pointing in the same direction as the runners instead of facing the runners as it was originally situated. Just over a mile beyond the statue is Heartbreak Hill, pictured below, whose namesake derives from the heartbreak Kelley suffered at the hands of Ellison "Tarzan" Brown at the 1936 race when Brown won and Kelley came in fifth. (Photos by Paul Clerici.)

The Boston Marathon Centennial Monument, shown above in Copley Square at the southeast corner of Dartmouth Street and Boylston Street, was dedicated April 9, 1996, as part of the 100th anniversary. The centerpiece is a 15-foot-diameter medallion which features the course, a list of each community along the route, and the 210 names and times of each men's and women's open, wheelchair, and masters winners etched in stone (subsequent winners are added). Pictured below are details of the granite bollards. Posts feature the BAA logo, a town seal from the course, a male runner, female runner, wheelchair athlete, and masters runners. (Photos by Paul Clerici.)

After the 2013 bombings, memorials and tributes popped up throughout the city. One of the main memorials in Boston grew at the east end of Boylston Street at Arlington Street, above. When Boylston Street and environs began to reopen, the memorial was moved to Copley Square, below. Flowers, running shoes, flags, handmade crosses, teddy bears, posters, and more were periodically collected, cleaned, and stored. While not a permanent memorial or monument, once the site was removed and the streets and Copley Square returned to normal, all the items were categorized and saved at the City of Boston Archives. (Photos by Paul Clerici.)

In 2016, three thin blue lines were painted on Boylston Street, pictured. They were painted in memory of the three victims of the 2013 bombings, and the color blue was chosen to honor the first responders and officers whose sworn duty is "separating good from evil," as noted by the Boston Police Department. (Photo by Paul Clerici.)

At left, the brick depicting running legs is 1 of 100 bronze bricks installed in 1985 as part of Kate Burke and Gregg Lefevre's "Boston Bricks: A Celebration of Boston's Past and Present." In 2000, Bill Rodgers was honored at the Faneuil Hall of Fame with bronze running shoes and plaque, at right. (Photos by Paul Clerici.)

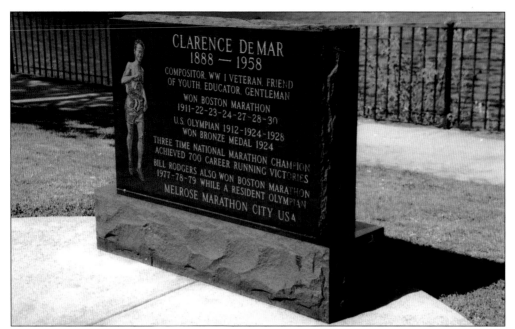

In Melrose, Massachusetts, Clarence DeMar is honored with this three-foot-tall, 1,100-pound monument. Also featured is Bill Rodgers with his Boston wins. GBTC coach Bill Squires brought his idea to fruition to honor the great runners, all of whom, including Squires, lived in Melrose. (Photo by Paul Clerici.)

Quad-City Times's Bix 7 in Iowa has Ted McElhiney–created statues of runners Joan Benoit Samuelson and Bill Rodgers for their combined six *Quad-City Times* Bix 7 wins. Dedicated in 1999, statues include, from left to right, supporter Dan Hayes, race director Ed Froehlich, musician Leon Bismark "Bix" Beiderbecke, and columnist Bill Wundram. (Photo by Toni Reavis.)

In Cape Cod, Massachusetts, two-time winner Johnny "The Elder" Kelley is honored at the Johnny Kelley Recreation Area in South Dennis with the Johnny Kelley Trail and a bust (left), dedicated in 1990. And at Roland C. Nickerson State Park in Brewster is a monument, dedicated in 1981. (Photo by Paul Clerici.)

Johnny "The Younger" Kelley, the 1957 winner, was honored in 2014 in Mystic, Connecticut, with the Brian Hanlon–created *Fast Friends* statue. From left to right, two-time winner Geoff Smith, 1968 winner Amby Burfoot, three-time winner Sara Mae Berman, four-time winner Bill Rodgers, 1972 winner Nina Kuscsik, and 1976 winner Jack Fultz. (Photo by Jim Roy.)

Onondaga Cogwagee Thomas Longboat, the 1907 winner, is honored in his native Canada. There are two plaques on Six Nations of the Grand River First Nation reserve in Ohsweken, Ontario. Pictured above, from left to right, are the Persons of National Historic Significance plaque at Gaylord Powless Arena and the Ontario Heritage Foundation historical marker at the former site of the Six Nations Council House. Pictured below, the *Challenge and Triumph* statue, created by David General, was dedicated at the 2015 Toronto Pan Am Games and then installed at its permanent location at the site of the Six Nations Community Hall and Gaylord Powless Arena. (Above, ontarioplaques.com; below, photo by Marco Manna.)

In Bandon, Ireland, is a monument for Ireland-born US Olympian John Lordan (Lorden in the United States) that reads, "John C. Lordan; Ballylangley, Bandon; Winner Boston Marathon 1903 and Olympian 1904; Born 26th June 1876; Erected by Bandon Athletic Club from Public Subscriptions; Unveiled by his Niece November 2000." (Bandon Athletic Club, County Cork, Ireland.)

While a large laminated finish line is installed for Marathon Monday, later in the week is when workers actually paint the Boston Marathon finish line. After Boylston Street is closed, large stencils are used, as seen here with highway safety traffic designers Will Belezos (left) and Eric House. (Photo by Paul Clerici.)

ABOUT THE AUTHOR

Paul C. Clerici—author of *A History of the Falmouth Road Race: Running Cape Cod, Boston Marathon History by the Mile, Journey of the Boston Marathon* (Chinese translation), and *History of the Greater Boston Track Club*—has been covering the sport of running and the Boston Marathon since the 1980s. Freelance journalist, photographer, lecturer, historian, cable television producer-host, and former award-winning newspaper editor and sports editor, he has been recognized by *Marquis Who's Who in the East* and received the Albert Nelson Marquis Lifetime Achievement Award. Often invited to be a guest on television and radio programs, he has written for numerous newspapers and magazines. Race director of the Camy 5K Run and David 5K Walk, he has competed in nearly every distance from the mile to the marathon, including 2 triathlons and 43 marathons (Boston Marathon 23 times). A Curry College and Walpole High School alumnus and Walpole High School Hall of Fame member, he resides in Massachusetts.

The "It All Starts Here" sign is found near the Boston Marathon's starting line in the center of Hopkinton and often serves as the backdrop for photographs. Pictured from left to right are brothers Frank Clerici Jr. and author Paul C. Clerici and their parents, Carol Hunt-Clerici and father Frank Clerici Sr. (Photo courtesy Paul Clerici.)

DISCOVER THOUSANDS OF LOCAL HISTORY BOOKS FEATURING MILLIONS OF VINTAGE IMAGES

Arcadia Publishing, the leading local history publisher in the United States, is committed to making history accessible and meaningful through publishing books that celebrate and preserve the heritage of America's people and places.

Find more books like this at
www.arcadiapublishing.com

Search for your hometown history, your old stomping grounds, and even your favorite sports team.